From Grandma D— ⌐⌐

Copyright © 2020 Sharon Deur

ISBN: 978-1-952369-13-1
LCCN: 2020911419

Published by EABooks Publishing a division of

Living Parables of Central Florida, Inc. a 501c3

EABooksPublishing.com

From Grandma D— ⌐⌐

VICTOR DISCOVERS TREASURE

45 Daily Devotional Digs for Kids

Book 1

Sharon Deur

Illustrated by Deborah Smith

 Check out Victor's Facebook page @victorthedonkey

To my precious mom,

Irene Potter.

In every chapter of the lives of your seven children, you made

us hungry and thirsty for God's Word.

Thank You for your example and your legacy of faith!

Table of Contents

Victor the Donkey	3
You Are God's Treasure	4
Is God Your Treasure	5
Shoulders Are For Resting	6
Shoulders (again)	7
Obey Road Signs	8
We are Clay Pots	9
We Are Cracked Clay Pots	10
I Am His Sheep	11
Sheep Habits	12
Tricky Wolf	13
The Trusty Gate	14
A Work of Art	15
Look At the Birds	16
A Loud Cluck and Strong Wings	17
Your Safe Place	18
Dwelling Place	19
Just Like Tents	20
Vines and Branches	21
Tree Talk	22
Be Fruity	23
Strong Deep Roots	24
Your Heart Has Eyes and Ears	25
Honey	26
Bright With Light	27
What Path Are You On?	28
Hide It!	29
Jesus Is Your Ladder	30
God and Gold	31
Rope and Anchor	32
Don't Forget The Soap	33
Living Water	34
Olive Tree	35
Wearing The Right Clothes?	36
Protect Yourself	37
Got Your Truth On?	38
Are You Living Right?	39
Ready, Set, Go!	40
You're Covered!	41
What are You Thinking?	42
Stay Sharp	43
Pray It On!	44
It's A Race To The Finish	45
We're On A Trip	46
Solid As A Rock	47
Special Prayer	48
Dig Deeper	49

Acknowledgements

I am humbled and honored to acknowldege God first! Solomon set the example in Proverbs 3:6: "In all your ways acknowledge him..." God planted the seeds for this book many years ago. *He* gave me the ideas. He's *my* Potter. He shapes *me* every day and He has allowed this book to take shape.

He has also put precious, praying people on my path to help me:

--my loving, patient husband, Dave, who encouraged and enabled me to flex my writing "muscles."

--my *amazing* children who inspired me, cheered me on, and helped with photography, technology, reading my first drafts, and giving physical support.

--my dear parents and all of my in-laws.

--my six incredible siblings.

--my *many* faithful, gentle friends.

--my author-friends, Renè Schmidt and Grace Gayle, who shared their experience and discerning wisdom.

--my former neighbors, Clint and Barb McGinnis, who adore their pet donkey, Roscoe. Through photos, emails, and letters they coached me on the varied characteristics, antics, and habits of donkeys.

--the 2016-17 fourth grade class of Fremont Christian School who listened and critiqued my first rough drafts when I was substitute teaching there for two weeks.

--all the students I taught over a 24 year span. They blessed me *daily* and motivated me to keep explaining Bible truths in a way that was meaningful to *them.*

--Crystal Bowman, author of more than 100 children's books, was the first one God used to redirect my story writing to *devotional* writing. She did this during Carol Kent's Speak Up Conference in 2018. She then edited this devotional with gracious, kind honesty and expertise. Her comments inspired me and kept driving me forward.

--Cheri, Debbie (illustrator), Bob (formatter), Tanya, Lily, Kristen, and Michelle, of EA Publishing were godly "coaches"--patient with me and thorough in their explanations. They were always just an email or a phone call away. Debbie truly depicted each biblical metaphor with excellence.

To *all* of you mentioned above, I thank you and I thank God *for* you! "May you be richly rewarded by the Lord...under whose wings you have come to take refuge." (Ruth 2:12)

Introduction

Treasure. Adventure. Gold. Eager to start hunting?

In this book Victor the donkey is going to help us dig up *word treasures* that God put in *His* Book, the Bible. *These are words that put a picture in our minds so we can remember them.*

Sometimes our parents and grandparents speak in *word treasures*:

If you hear, "It's a piece of cake", the *hidden* treasure meaning is that it is *easy* to do.

If they say, "They're all ears," the *hidden* treasure meaning is they were excited listeners.

"You're as hungry as a bear" means you act like you're *starving* in treasure language.

This book is meant to be a map; a guide to discover and explore Bible treasures like this:
God calls you and me pots, *sheep, branches,* salt. *He* is called a Rock, a Vine, Bread, Shepherd, Gate, Light.

God wants to get us thinking about Him and live in ways that put a big smile on His face! Our "gold" after all the treasure digging is living on earth *trusting* in a Jesus we cannot see *and* someday living in Heaven *with* Jesus looking at Him face to face!

Victor the donkey will not appear on *every* page, but Bible Treasure Talk *will*!
"Victor" is a *pretend* name for a *real* animal that we read about more than 100 times in the Bible! One time--are you ready for this?--a donkey talked! Oh, God is *full* of surprises.

The Bible says in Isaiah 45:3 (MSG), "I'll lead you to buried treasures..." Thanks for "digging" with me!

Note to Parents & Grandparents: In Romans 6 Paul describes our new lives in Christ as *freedom* from being slaves of sin and serving a *new* Master. Then in verse 19 (from THE MESSAGE) Paul says, "I'm using this freedom language because it's easy to picture." THAT is the purpose of this devotional! Making the language of the Bible and following Jesus "easy to picture"! I know you share in my heart's desire to help your children understand the gospel message *and* Jesus' Kingdom metaphors so that they are drawn into a tighter relationship with Him!

When you see   , it refers to the Bible passage(s) that supports that particular devotional. It's the "*Dig Deeper Bible Truth*" (*shovels* and *treasure* are just meant to be together). In the back of this devotional all the Dig Deeper Bible Truths are written out. The versions used were prayerfully selected according to what young children can understand most easily. The   indicates an *action*/activity the children are encouraged to do to give practical application to the truth explained.

MEET JESUS

A Miracle Baby;
A Miracle –Worker!

Son of God--
The God Who made this world
and <u>you</u>!

Invisible, but oh so
Real!

Made Blind
people see!

Loves us sooooo much that He
died on a cross for us!

Our Best Friend Forever
(BFF)
He's crazy about you!

Made lame
people walk!

Full of Kindness!

He Walked on Water!

Lived on Earth for a
while, **now** in Heaven
<u>and</u> in hearts! ♡
Yup! He's King of
the Universe, but
chooses to live in
our hearts! ♡
AMAZING!

Our
Leader
through
life!

Heart
Changer!
Heart Filler!

Best and <u>Only</u> Eraser
of our sins!

MEET VICTOR

Dependable!

Smart!

Calm!

Strong!

Friendly!

Guards Sheep!

Sure-footed!

Victor the Donkey

What does Victor the Donkey have to do with Treasure? Why will you see and hear his name in this book? These are good questions.

When Jesus was on this earth--after he grew up--a very special day came when Jesus rode into a big city called Jerusalem. There were no cars or trucks to ride in, so He chose a *donkey* to ride on. A donkey is a quiet, gentle animal.

That special donkey was carrying Jesus--a*n incredible Treasure for you and me!*

There were many children and grown-ups shouting, "YAY! Here comes the King!"

Some people who were not so nice said they should be quiet. Jesus replied, "If they are quiet the *stones* will shout out praise!" Are you picturing *that* in your mind? *That* shows how special Jesus was and is.

So since a donkey got to carry Jesus, a *donkey* often will explain the Bible treasures that you will read about in this book. Just remember, *Jesus* is the most important treasure *EVER!*

It's fun to give a *real* animal--chosen by Jesus--a *pretend* name...*Victor!*

Treasure Talk: A special donkey carried a Special Passenger.

 Luke 19:28-40

 Go outside. Shout, (really SHOUT): "YAY, Jesus. You're <u>my</u> King!"

3

You are God's Treasure!

God must love that word "treasure." He calls *you* His treasure. And *He* is yours. His Book, the Bible, is a treasure *map* to find out—to explore--more about Him.

 "GOD chose you out of all the people on Earth as his cherished personal **treasure**." Deut. 7:6 (MSG)

 "God Almighty will be your **treasure**, more wealth than you can imagine." Job 22:25 (MSG)

 "God's Word warns us of danger and directs us to hidden **treasure**." Ps. 19:11 (MSG)

Are there some days when you don't feel very special? Maybe at school no one chose *you* to play with or to be on their team? Maybe your brother or sister wouldn't share their toys.

Let's remember that what God thinks of us matters the most.
He *treasures* you (that means He's crazy about you). He even knows what you *think*.

He knows what you say *before* you say it.

What does God want *you* to do?
Believe in Him. Love Him. Obey Him. Pray to Him. You don't need fancy words. Just talk to Him like you would a friend. *He cares!*

Treasure Talk: To God you are a special treasure.

 Psalm 139:1-6

 Say thank you to God for making YOU His treasure!

Is God Your Treasure?

What do you think about the most? Whatever your answer is, *that* is what you treasure.

Those things may be good things. God just wants us to think about Him, His Son, Jesus, and His Heaven **more**. A

Money, games, TV, sports, jewelry, clothes, and fun are things we *see* with our eyes or *do* with our hands and feet, and we think NOTHING could be better.

Look again *here* at the Dig Deeper Bible Truth: "The place where your treasure is, is the place you will most want to be, and end up being" (Matthew 6:21).

Jesus wants us to end up in Heaven with Him. <u>That</u> will be better than gold! B

Treasure Talk: Give God the MOST important place in your thought-list.

A Matt. 6:19-21
B Matt. 13:44-46

Draw a picture of what you treasure most. THEN put a large **G O D** right over top of it with a thick marker or crayon.

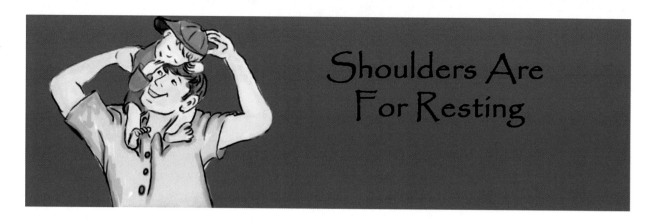

Shoulders Are For Resting

Ever see a baby ride in a back pack on Mom or Dad? Where does their head land if they fall asleep? Right! Between Mom's or Dad's shoulders. That must feel so good. The baby feels warm, safe, and loved.

God's Book says: "The one the Lord loves rest between His shoulders." A

Jesus loves YOU! He wants you to know that just as a baby rests his head between Mom's or Dad's shoulders, *you* can feel *that* good when you love Jesus back.

That kind of love makes you want to talk to Him about good things *and* not-so-good things.

Not-so-good things can feel heavy. Victor knows what heavy feels like when he carries loads of pots or food.

When the load comes off, Victor feels better, moves faster, and goes farther.

You will feel better (warm, safe, and loved) when you give your loads to Jesus.

Do this by just talking to Him about it...that's called prayer. B, C

Treasure Talk: It feels good to talk to God about anything and everything.

DIG DEEPER

A Deut. 33:12
B Psalm 55:22
C Matt. 11:28

Tell God about a not-so-good thing in your life. Let Him carry it for you!

Shoulders (again)

Look what God put on Victor's back.

A CROSS--between his shoulders and along his spine.

Amazing! Our Great God, Who loves us and carries our loads, lets the shape of the cross show up on many donkeys' backs!

Before Jesus was nailed to a cross He *sat* on the form of one.

God hides incredible treasures on or inside creatures or things He made:

Apples have a star inside. Jesus is called the Morning Star.

The Sailcat fish skeleton looks like Jesus on the cross

What an amazing, full-of-wonder-God we have!

Treasure Talk: Hints about God show up in nature.

A   Job 12:7-9
B   Rev. 22:16
C   Phil. 2:8-11

Ask Dad or Mom to cut an apple in half for you so you can see the star inside! Thank Jesus for hiding this treasure in a piece of fruit! With help, press half of the apple into red paint and then onto a paper towel.☺

Obey Road Signs

Victor is excited to tell you of that time when a donkey *talked* in the Bible: A

A man we will call Mr. B was riding a donkey. Mr. B was on his way to meet with a bad king in order to say bad things about some good people. God did *not* want him to do this, so He put a special angel right smack in the middle of the road **3** different times. Mr. B could *not* see the angel, but the donkey *could*. God was trying to stop him from talking with this bad king. Each time the donkey refused to keep going! Each time Mr. B got very upset. After the third time, the donkey *spoke*! She said, "What have I done to make you so angry with me these three times?"

Mr. B answered the donkey, "You've been playing games with me! I'm mad at you!"

The donkey said to Mr. B, "Aren't I your trusty donkey? You've ridden me for years! Have I *ever* done anything like this to you before? Have I?"

"No," said Mr. B.

Then the Lord opened Mr. B's eyes and he saw the angel in the middle of the road.

Kids, when adults are driving, there are special road signs they must obey: stop signs, yield signs, and railroad crossing signs. Trouble can happen if drivers don't obey them! Sometimes God stops **us** from making poor choices. He stops us by letting something *else* happen instead. We may get angry or be very sad. But because God loves us, He is keeping us from getting hurt or making a big mistake.

"Road signs" are called "*warnings*" in God's Treasure Book, the Bible. B

When we don't get our way--instead of getting mad---let's say, "Thank You, God. I know *Your* way is best!"

Treasure Talk: Things don't just happen; they're planned by God.

A Num. 22:21-35
B Psalm 19:11

Talk about a time when your plans did not work out. Thank Jesus for that!

We are Clay Pots

When Jesus lived on earth, pots were made of the *clay* that people dug up from the ground. They shaped it with their hands on a special wheel. They dried it in a hot oven, and filled it with water or food.

[Donkeys carried *many* heavy clay pots when Jesus lived on earth]

God calls us *pots* in the Bible. It's okay! Remember, the Bible uses many word pictures to help us understand something important.

A carpenter builds houses. An artist paints or draws. A cook makes tasty things to eat. *A potter makes pots!*

If *the Bible calls us "pots,"* guess who our Potter is? YES! It's GOD!

A clay pot is *carefully* shaped into *exactly* what the potter wants to use it for. 🪏A

YOU were created for a reason—shaped *carefully*—not with clay—but with skin, bones, muscles, and brains. 🪏B

When potters on earth are done making a pot, they admire its beauty and its purpose.

When the *Expert Potter*—God—makes *us*, He keeps on shaping and re-shaping us *every* day, and *every* day He steps back and says, "He is just right!" "She is just right!"

He has a plan for you at *this* age AND He knows what you will be when you grow up!

Treasure Talk: God forms and shapes you *exactly* right.

DIG DEEPER

A Jer. 18:3,4
B Psalm 139:13-16

Using Play-Doh® or clay, make a small pot. Shape it and smooth it until you just love it! Now you know how God feels about <u>you</u>, His incredible, special "pot!" Thank Him for how He made you!

We are Cracked Clay Pots

Sure hope you dug deeper yesterday and read Jeremiah 18:3 & 4.

Read it again. Look at the part that says," He was making a pot from clay. But something went wrong with it..."

That means the "pot"—you and me—**sinned.** We did something wrong that our Potter has to fix. And let's face it—we sin every single day, more than once.

Ask yourself, "Did I disobey my parents or teachers? Was I unkind to someone? Did I tell a lie? Did I *think* about something I know is wrong? Did I use angry words? Was I lazy?"

If you can say yes to any of those questions then you are a *cracked pot.*

HERE IS THE BEST NEWS OF ALL—If we ask God to forgive us—to erase—our sin,

HE DOES!

That's Him smoothing our "cracks" EVERY day.

And they disappear forever. God can do that because He sent His only Son, Jesus, to pay for our sins by dying on a cross. AMAZING LOVE! LOVING POTTER!

Treasure Talk: God's the only One Who can forgive our sins.

 1 John 1:9

 Make another pot! This time use a pencil point to make a crack in it. Every time you look at it ask God to erase the cracks in your life and say, "Thank You, God, for being the Expert Potter Who smooths out my sin-filled cracks every day because of the love of Jesus!"

10

I Am His Sheep

Victor wants us to know that donkeys are animal experts when it comes to knowing sheep.

One of the many jobs that donkeys do best is *guard* flocks of sheep, so they don't get into danger or trouble.

In the Bible we are called God's *sheep.* A

So, if we are God's sheep and a farmer who takes care of sheep is called a *shepherd*, guess Who the Shepherd is in treasure talk?

You've got it...God. Jesus. The Bible calls *Him* the **Good** Shepherd. B

Regular shepherds can't be everywhere all the time, so they use *donkeys* to help protect the sheep from bigger animals.

Jesus doesn't need any help protecting us.

He's a GREAT, BIG, POWERFUL, ALL-SEEING Shepherd! C

Treasure Talk: God loves us and knows us just as a shepherd loves and knows his sheep.

A Psalm 100:3
B John 10:11
C Job 34:21

Glue some cotton balls onto paper so it looks like a sheep. Below your sheep write, "I am Jesus' sheep!" HE is my Shepherd!

Sheep Habits

Here are more ways that *we* are **like** a sheep and *Jesus* is **like** a Shepherd:

A shepherd takes care of his sheep ⟶ God takes care of us. A

Sheep need a LOT of help ⟶ *There are LOTS of things only God can help us with.* B

Where the shepherd leads, the sheep follow. ⟶ If we don't follow Jesus, who ARE we following? C

Sheep recognize their own shepherd's call ⟶ We just KNOW when Jesus is speaking to us. D

The shepherd feeds them; the sheep eat. ⟶ The Bible is our food. Are we gobbling it up? E

If a sheep gets lost, the shepherd searches until he finds it ⟶ If we decide not to obey and love Jesus, He won't give up on us until we decide we *want* to be His sheep again. F

Treasure Talk: God protects us, leads us, guides us.

A Psalm 23:1
B Heb. 13:5, 6
C John 10:27
D John 10:3
E Jer. 15:16
F Luke 15:3-7

The treasure pile is REALLY deep today with SIX golden Bible verses! Read them over and over until you KNOW, yes REALLY KNOW you are God's sheep. The Bible says so! YAHOO!

A Tricky Wolf

Wolves are enemies of sheep. Donkeys help protect sheep from them. The Bible calls Satan a wolf because he is *our* number one enemy.

A *real* wolf wants to gobble up a tasty, sweet, gentle lamb or sheep.

In Bible treasure talk, Satan wants to gobble up any thoughts we have about Jesus.

He doesn't want us to think about Him or believe in Him or His Bible.

WHAT A WOLF!

Satan dresses up in lies. A

If someone tells you it is okay to steal, THAT is one of Satan's lies.

If you get angry very quickly and say bad words, it's almost as if Satan is telling you "That's okay; you want your way don't you?"

What about being selfish? That's Satan whispering to your heart, "You have every right to have that."

When you hear a lie going on, just whisper *this* name: **Jesus.**

Jesus will destroy that tricky lie and whisper His truth to you! B

Treasure talk: Satan is a pretender and liar. Jesus is Real.

A John 8:44
B John 14:6

If you think you've lied recently, tell God about it and then tell Mom or Dad. Your heart will feel like doing a happy dance!

The Trusty Gate

We have learned that donkeys help protect sheep from enemies. To do that well, there must be a good *fence*.

Good fences need a *gate—like a door—*to let the sheep in and out.

We are *like* sheep; Jesus is our Shepherd. A The enemy is Satan and anyone who lies to us. The *fence* is God's Words to us.

If we <u>know</u> and <u>obey</u> God's words, we will have the <u>key</u> that *keeps the enemy out!*

The Gate is Jesus. He is ours. We are His.
Jesus protects His sheep, and keeps the enemy out. YAHOO!

"Don't fear little flock. Your Father wants to give you the kingdom." B

Jesus is the **ONLY WAY** for His sheep (us) to get into His Heaven.

THAT IS BECAUSE HE DIED ON A CROSS TO ERASE OUR SINS!

🅞 [Stop reading right now and "Dig Deeper" C to read God's Words!]

Treasure Talk: We must believe in Jesus to enter His Heaven someday.

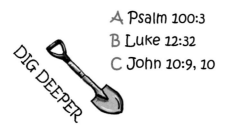

A Psalm 100:3
B Luke 12:32
C John 10:9, 10

Sometimes "Door" is used instead of "Gate". **Gently** open and close the door to the outside of your house. Thank Jesus for being your One and Only Door to Heaven!

A Work Of Art

Have you ever burst through the door and said, "Mom! Dad! Look what I made!"

God says that about *you every single minute of every single day:*

"Look what I made! I made a Masterpiece! A

It is perfect! I wouldn't change a thing!"

Yes, y*ou* are God's *treasure*.

Yes, you are one of His sheep.

Yes, you are a smoothed out incredible *pot.*

And Yes! You are God's *masterpiece*—a work of art that would hang on God's refrigerator (if He had one).

Treasure Talk: It is what *God* thinks about you that matters most.

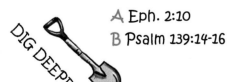 A Eph. 2:10
B Psalm 139:14-16

Say this out loud (not shouting, but really loud)! "I praise you because you made me in an amazing and wonderful way. What you have done is wonderful. I know this very well. You saw my bones being formed as I took shape in my mother's body. When I was put together there, you saw my body as it was formed. All the days planned for me were written in your book before I was one day old." B

Look at the Birds

Once there was a hummingbird trapped in a garage. The big door was open but it didn't know how to get out. It kept flying around near the ceiling.

The dad who lived at that house got a ladder and very carefully caught the bird. He held it in his hands until he could bring it outside.

Before he let it go, he gave his children a close-up look at the tiny hummingbird. He told them that *Jesus* once said to His followers, "Look at the birds." ✎A

Jesus (and that special dad) knew that birds have something to teach us.

They don't worry about stuff like we do. They fly around, eat bugs or seeds, make nests, and whistle special songs without even *thinking* about it.

If one bird falls out of its nest, God knows about it. WOW! ✎B

He knew that the hummingbird couldn't find its way out of a garage.

But here's the best part—If God knows when a *bird* falls (or gets trapped), just think about how much He cares for YOU—a *person* He made! He even knows EXACTLY how many hairs are on your head! ✎B

Treasure Talk: God cares for you right down to counting the hairs on your head.

A Matt. 6:26
B Matt. 10:29-30

Your turn—start counting how many hairs are on Mom or Dad's head (or a brother's or sister's). When did you give up counting?
Think about this: God just KNOWS without *even* counting!

16

A Loud Cluck and Strong Wings

Today Victor is visiting his donkey cousins on a farm. Horses and goats are in the pasture, and a flock of chicks are running around while a mother hen watches.

It is fun to watch a mother hen with her little chicks. They follow her so closely. If there is *any* danger at all—a dog, a hawk, a fox—the mama hen will use her loud cluck and her mighty wings to protect her chicks. The chicks know her special cluck and will gather underneath her.

A mother hen protects her chicks no matter what. If there's a fire, a thunderstorm, or a wild animal on the loose, she will spread her wings over her chicks so they will be safe. God created hens that way, and He uses that idea to show us how much He loves us.

Treasure Talk: Jesus wants to gather His children together (that's you!) as a hen gathers her chicks under her wings.

He loves us so much that He would even die for us! *And He did!*

 Matt. 23:37

Since Jesus has *arms* and not *wings*, ask one of your parents or grandparents to hold you in a *special* hug that makes you feel safe. THAT is the *"mind photo"* God gives us of Himself in Deuteronomy 33:27—"The everlasting God is your place of safety. His arms will hold you up forever."

That's God-Love!

Your Safe Place

You learned that chicks feel safe under their mother's wings. Other barnyard animals feel safe when there is a fence and a closed gate. This makes *people* on the farm feel safer too 😊 .

Victor feels safe when he has a covered pen to *sleep* in at night and a place where he can stand when the weather gets bad.

What makes *you* feel safe? Do you feel safe when your parents or grandparents are with you? Do you feel safe when you know the doors are all locked?

It's good to be careful and make wise decisions so we can stay safe, but if you ever feel afraid or alone, remember that God is with you and you can call out to Him to help you.

Here are some great verses to help you feel safe:

"…GOD became my hideout; God was my high mountain retreat." A

And

"His huge outstretched arms protect you—
under them you're perfectly safe;
his arms fend off all harm.
Fear nothing…Yes, because GOD's your refuge,

the High God your very own home." B

Treasure Talk: Ask God to keep you safe and remember He is always near.

A Psalm 94:22
B Psalm 91:4,9
C Heb. 13:5,6

Okay, now read this! It's a treasure but not mystery talk. God says it plain & simple: [Say it out LOUD]

"I'll never let you down, never walk off and leave you," … 'God is there, ready to help; I'm fearless no matter what. Who or what can get to me?'" C

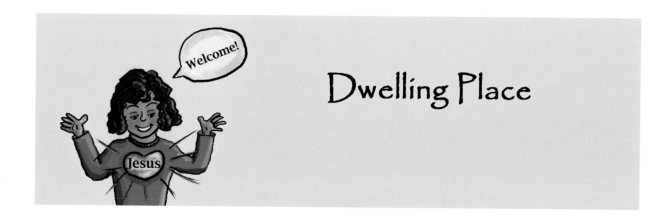

Dwelling Place

"Well, that's a strange title", you may be thinking.

Think of the address of your house—*that* is <u>your</u> *dwelling place*—the place where you live with your family.

God calls <u>us</u> His dwelling place. ⛏A *He lives in us!* He controls what we think, what we do, and what we say.

If we believe God is real,

if we believe that Jesus is God's Son,

if we believe that Jesus died on a cross to save us from our sins,

THEN God's Spirit lives (dwells) in us AND we get to live (dwell) in His Heaven when we die! ⛏B

The Bible tells us that God's Holy *Spirit* lives **in** us—His special children. ⛏C

The Holy Spirit helps us know right from worng. He reminds us that God is with us and He helps us to be kind to others.

[🛑 right now and shout, "THANK YOU, GOD!"].

Treasure Talk: God's Spirit lives in you to be your Helper.

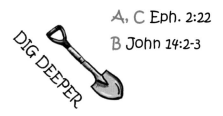

A, C Eph. 2:22

B John 14:2-3

If God's Holy Spirit lives in us, let's make it a welcoming place! Begin by thinking & talking well about yourself--without bragging.

Just Like Tents

In the Bible many people were shepherds and lived in tents. They had to move often to find fresh green pastures and water for their flocks. They had to keep putting up tents or take them down. It was sort of like camping all the time.

Victor and his friends were used to seeing tents. They often had to guard the sheep and carry heavy loads to help their owners move from one place to another.

Because God knew all this, He used "tents" in His treasure talk about our *bodies*:

"Our bodies are **like tents** that we live in here on earth." A

Now *real* tents get old, get holes, get kind of smelly...they just wear out.

Our bodies also get old and someday when we die, we will get *new* bodies and a brand *new* Home in Heaven. God also calls THAT home a "dwelling place." It won't be a building that someone built, but it will be beautiful and it will be big! B

Treasure Talk: God created our bodies where His Spirit lives.

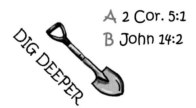

A 2 Cor. 5:1
B John 14:2

Tents need poles or chairs to keep it up and keep it strong! Are you keeping your body— your "tent" strong by exercising and eating healthy? Stand in front of a mirror. Flex your muscles and say, "What a good-looking tent you are!"

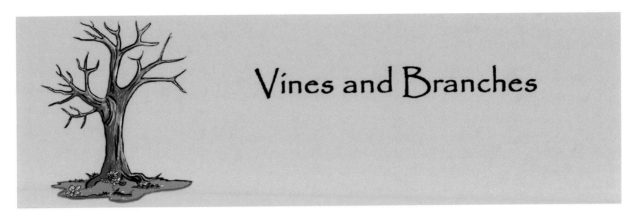

Vines and Branches

After a big windstorm, Dad or Mom may ask you to go in the yard and pick up sticks and branches that have shaken loose from the trees. Do they ask you to try to stick them back into the tree? Of course not; it's impossible!

Those branches are gathered up and thrown into a pile to rot or burn. *They cannot live without the tree and its trunk.*

The trunk acts like a semi-truck to carry water and vitamins from the roots to the leaves and fruit.

Jesus didn't use the word *trunk*. He calls it a *vine*. A *vine* growing fruit or veggies is just as important as the *trunk* of a tree. If you remove the fruit from the *vine* it shrivels up and dies.

Jesus said, "I am the vine, you are the branches."

We have to stay connected to Jesus, or our joy dies.

HOW? Pray to Him.
> Listen to His Words in the Bible when you hear them or read them.
> > Listen to your parents or teachers when they talk about Jesus.
> > > Talk to your friends about Him.
> > > > Pray some more. Prayer is an instant semi-truck to Jesus.

Treasure Talk: If we stay stuck to Jesus, we will keep growing.

John 15:5-8

Try to find a branch with leaves out in the yard. Count the number of days it takes for the leaves to die. How long can you last without Jesus? Read all of John 15:5-8 in "Dig Deeper". Draw a picture of a simple tree. Put the name, "Jesus" on the Trunk. Put <u>your</u> name and your family members' names on the branches.

Tree Talk

Yesterday you learned that we are like branches connected to the "Trunk"--Jesus!

It is exciting to know that the Bible's Treasure Map also calls us *trees*. ✎A

A strong young tree that grows in your yard needs good **dirt**, lots of **sunshine**, and just the right amount of **water**.

Growing as a Christian doesn't need *real* dirt, sunshine, and water.

We grow as Jesus' children by **listening** to the Bible's words, *thinking* about them, **obeying** them, and **praying** to Him about *everything*.

And saying "Thank You" to Him a LOT! ✎B

If we do those things, we will be sinking our roots in Jesus, and growing good and important "fruit" (that's tomorrow's subject).

AND our "leaves" won't shrink up (leaves only shrink when they don't get enough water or sunlight).

Treasure Talk: Be alive with actions that please Jesus.

A Psalm 1:2-3
B Col. 2:6-7

Inside every leaf is a nature *factory* that keeps leaves green! Green means alive! Draw a leaf. Color it green. Write these words on the leaf: **pray, obey, listen**—factory-type words that keep you alive in Jesus!

Be Fruity

An apple orchard has trees that only grow apples. An orange grove has trees that only grow oranges. God designed fruit to grow best that way.

For just a minute though, let's pretend you're inside a one-of-a-kind orchard where *every* fruit tree is different.

You'd constantly point and say, "There's an apple tree! There's an orange tree! There's a pear tree!" The shape and color of the fruit lets you know what kind of tree it is. If Victor's relatives were with you, they'd love it if you'd throw them an apple or pear once in a while.

You have learned that the Bible calls people who love and obey God *good trees.* Since we are called "trees," our "fruit" is our actions. What we ***do*** shows what we are like.
A

Our fruit shows up in: B

Love	Patience	Faithfulness
Joy	Kindness	Gentleness
Peace	Goodness	Self-control

Jesus says, "By their fruits you will know them."   C

Treasure Talk: Is my life being fruit-full?

A Prov. 20:11
B Gal. 5:22
C Matt. 7:16

There are 9 "fruits" listed above...how can you show those "fruits"? Can your friends tell what kind of "tree" you are?

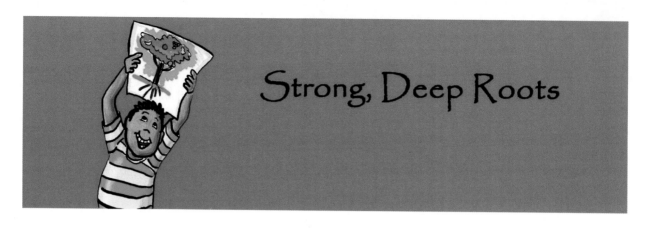

Strong, Deep Roots

Tree roots go down *below* the soil as far as the tree shoots up *above* the soil. Those roots are needed for the tree to stay living, standing, and strong.

If the roots die, the tree dies. Roots are like *roads* that carry the vitamins and water from the soil to the rest of the tree.

You now know that God's mystery talk calls us trees and branches and our lives must grow fruit.

Trusting in Jesus is just like vitamin water! Since we are a tree that grows fruit we *cannot* live without Jesus—just like a tree cannot grow without its roots!

Treasure Talk: The more you pray and the more you listen to God's Words, the stronger you will be.

Jer. 17:7-8

Draw a big picture of a tree including branches, fruit, and roots (it doesn't have to be fancy or perfect). Write "JESUS" on the trunk with a red marker. Write your name on a branch with a blue marker. Draw 9 colorful fruits somewhere on the branches and write each of the fruits on them (yes, of course you can ask for help!) Right over top of the roots with a green marker, write, "God's Word", "God's Love", "Prayer"

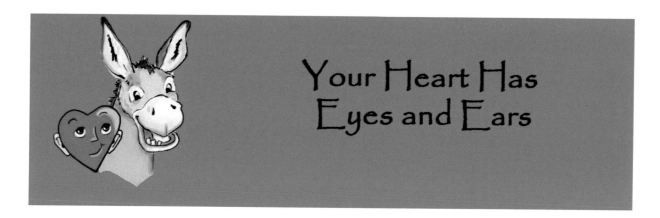

Your Heart Has Eyes and Ears

Look carefully at this picture of Victor.
The two things that make donkeys cute are their eyes and their ears.
Their eyes are large and have a gentle, sleepy look to them.
Their ears are very tall. They help a donkey hear things that are miles away.

Jesus says something very interesting about eyes and ears:

"God has blessed you, because your eyes can see, and your ears can hear!" A

Jesus is not talking about our body's REAL eyes and ears—He's talking about the eyes and ears of our **hearts** where His Spirit lives!
Our hearts and our minds are connected. We were created to make choices with our brains. But those choices begin in our hearts.
It's what is in *there* that makes us *chose* to love Jesus, listen to Jesus, and talk about

Jesus. B

That is reason to shout, **"YAHOO!** I know Jesus! I have a Dad or a Mom, a Grandpa or Grandma, a teacher or a friend that *told* me about Jesus and now my heart's eyes and ears are sharp. **YAHOO AGAIN!"**

Treasure Talk: Keep testing your heart's vision and hearing.

A Matt. 13:16
B Luke 6:45

Who do you know that does NOT know Jesus in his or her heart? Write their name here_____
Be their hero and friend and tell them that Jesus loves them too! It will take the blindfold _off_ and the earplugs _out_ of their heart! ☺

Honey Talk

When hearing that word, "honey" it may make your mouth water. Honey is sweet and tasty. It makes toast terrific, cereal scrumptious, and milk magnificent.

Honey can sometimes help to heal coughs in your throat and pain on your skin!

Here's the Bible's treasure about honey:

> "Kind words are like honey—
>
> they cheer you up and make you feel strong."

Kind words make you feel good when you *hear* them and good when you *say* them.

Words spoken to parents, grandparents, and teachers, should ALWAYS be respectful, but *test* your words when you speak with brothers, sisters, and friends.
Use the **T.H.I.N.K.** Test:

Are your words: <u>T</u>rue? <u>H</u>elpful? <u>I</u>mportant? <u>N</u>eeded? <u>K</u>ind?

If your words pass this test, guess Who is the *happiest*? Yes→**JESUS!**

Treasure Talk: How sweet are your words?

 Prov. 16:24

 With permission take a taste of honey right now. Are you smiling and smacking your lips?
Let EVERYONE who "tastes" <u>your</u> words smile just as big!

Bright With Light

When the electricity goes out during a storm, we reach for a flashlight or a candle. We want to be able to see what we're doing and where we're going. Why be in the dark if we don't have to?

Jesus said, "I am the Light of the world. Whoever follows me will never walk in darkness but will have the light of life." A

Light and darkness do not mix. If we listen to Satan's lies it's like living in the dark. Only Jesus, our Light, can smash the dark and make our lives bright again. B Light leads and guides. Jesus leads and guides us. *He* makes us smart when it comes to choices we have to make.

A cord has to be plugged in for a lamp to give light. We MUST stay "plugged into" Jesus. THEN we have the Light of Life!

Treasure Talk: Jesus is like Light that takes away the dark.

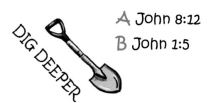

A John 8:12
B John 1:5

With an adult, take a flashlight and go into the darkest room of the house or into a closet with the light turned off. Sit there in the dark for just a few seconds. Then turn on the flashlight. Now say, "There, Satan, take THAT! *Jesus* is the *Light* that lives in me!"

What Path Are You On?

Pretend you're on a hike at night with Dad or Mom. You've got a light to shine on the path you are following. You need to see where you are going so you don't trip and fall.

God's calls our whole life a "path."

A path always leads somewhere. Our path on this earth leads to Heaven!

We've learned that Jesus is the Light of the world and He uses the Bible to shine light on our path. ⛏A

The Bible *lights up our path,* so we keep our eyes on Jesus. ⛏B

Here's more Bible treasure-talk about our "path":

Following Jesus is a path of *peace.* ⛏C Following Jesus is the *right* path. ⛏D

Treasure Talk: Life is like a path. God and His Bible keep us on the right one.

A Psalm 119:105
B Heb. 12:2
C Luke 1:79
D Ps. 23:3

Name the people in your life right now who love Jesus and who are walking His path-way with you. (Dig Deeper into the Bible's Light)

Hide It!

When you *hide* something that is very special to *you*, you find a secret place for it. You are protecting it because you *care* about it!

The Bible says we should hide *God's Word* in our hearts. A

To hide it you have to **memorize** it—no, not the whole Bible--just verses that are special to *you*. Sometimes it's called "learning it by heart."

If you learn Bible verses "by heart," you will *never* forget them. You won't have to say, "Hmmm, now where did I put those words?" No! They just become part of who you are.

And those special verses become like gold to you; yes—*Treasure.*

Bury it deep inside. It will NOT get lost! B

Treasure Talk: Put God's Word in your mind and heart so it stays there.

 A Psalm 119:11
B Prov. 2:1-5

 Let's get started!
Learn <u>this</u> verse by heart:
"I will praise you, Lord,
with all my heart."
(The "address" is Psalm 138:1)

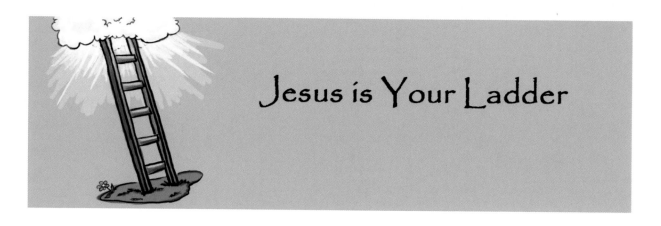

Jesus is Your Ladder

A ladder helps us get from a lower place to a higher one.

It takes a bit of work—reaching with our hands, stepping up with our feet and legs.

But when we get to the top it feels so good to say, "I made it!"

Jesus wants so much for *you* to go from this earth to His Heaven someday.

And believing in Him is the ONLY way to get there! A

In the New Testament of the Bible, Jesus is called a "Ladder." B

In the Old Testament of the Bible a man named Jacob took a nap in a field using a *rock* for a pillow *(OUCH!).* Jacob then had a dream. In his dream he saw God at the

top of a long ladder and angels were going up and coming down the ladder. C

Angels are God's messengers. What God says, they do.

When Jesus came to earth (Christmas), He came as God the Father's *Messenger*--to do as His Father asked—die for our sins (Good Friday) and then live again (Easter). And if we believe that, then we will see God in His Heaven when we die (shout THANK YOU, JESUS!).

THAT is why Jesus is called a Ladder--*HE brings US to God!*

Treasure Talk: Jesus is the help we need to get to God.

A John 14:6
B John 1:51
C Gen. 28:12

If you have help and permission, climb a short ladder. Otherwise just stare at one that is in your garage. As you climb or stare, say a prayer of thanks to Jesus for being your Ladder!

God and Gold

In this book you're holding right now we are digging for treasure!

We are discovering all kinds of treasures, but since a chest of gold appears at the bottom of each page, let's talk about **gold** for a minute!

Gold is shiny. Gold is beautiful to look at. Gold costs a lot.

People don't think there is ANYTHING better than gold. Ah, but there is:

Your faith in God! A   God's decisions! B   God's wisdom! C

Those things ARE better than gold while we live on this earth, but did you know that when we get to Heaven we will walk on *streets* of gold? D AMAZING!

But in Heaven it won't be the *gold* that makes us jump-up-and-down-happy!

GOD IS OUR TREASURE! Our eyes will be on Him! E

Treasure Talk: God is far more valuable than gold.

DIG DEEPER

A 1 Peter 1:7
B Psalm 19:9, 10
C Prov. 16:16
D Rev. 21:21
E Job 22:25

Today you'll need a gold crayon or paint and a black piece of paper.
In BIG letters write G O D on the paper. Put it where you will see it every day!

Rope and Anchor

A boat needs an anchor. It is something solid and heavy that's attached to the boat with a rope. If there is a strong wind or huge waves, an anchor is thrown overboard to keep the boat from floating away. It makes the boat owner feel much better!

An anchor gives hope to the captain that his boat is safe.

"Hope" and "Rope" rhyme! That makes it easy to remember that God is our Hope! If we grab hold of Him—love Him, pray to Him, obey Him, worship Him—then He saves us! He brings us to live with Him someday in His Heaven—just like an anchor in a storm saves a boat.

"Strong winds" or "huge waves" are mystery talk for *troubles* in our lives. What troubles *you*? Sickness? Hunger? Mean kids? Hard work at school? Parents fighting? Parents divorced?

GRAB HOLD of the ROPE of HOPE, TREASURE SEEKERS!
GOD IS YOUR ANCHOR!

Those troubles may not disappear, but God will help you REMEMBER and KNOW that He is THE Captain, that He is in control, and that He loves you no matter what!

Treasure Talk: Let God be your Anchor in life's storms.

 A Heb. 6:18-19

Draw an anchor like this

Draw a rope that goes through the hole on the top. With help use a thick marker to write on it: **God is my Anchor!**

Don't Forget the Soap

"Wash your hands." "Let's wash the car." "Time to do the laundry."
All of those cleaning jobs need **soap**! Soap *cleans* people or things.
We like things to be clean.

Long before washing machines were made--Victor and his friends were often used to carry heavy baskets of laundry down to the river so they could be cleaned (imagine how heavy those wet clothes were on the way back).

There are many times in the Bible where God talks about washing up! Yes, with soap and water, A, *but His "clean talk" is also mystery language. Soap cannot clean our* hearts! *Believing in Jesus can!* B
When Jesus died on the cross for our sins, He bled.

His blood—like soap—makes our hearts *clean*! C, D
That means when we die and go to God, He will say, "Ahhh, I know what's in your clean heart. I know that you believe in Me. I know that you believe in my Son, Jesus, who died for your sins. Come on into my Heaven! E

Treasure Talk: Jesus bled to scrub our hearts clean.

A Gen.43:24
B Psalm 51:7
C Lev.17:11
D Mal.3:2,3
E Matt.25:21

Let's put two treasures together! *"But if we live in the light, as God does, we share in life with each other. And the blood of his Son Jesus washes all our sins away."* Just for fun hold **soap** in one hand and a **flashlight** in the other!
Now read 1 John 1:7 (above) out loud.

Living Water

Can water be alive? Only in God's treasure language!

Besides using water to *clean*, we need to *drink* water to *live.* Victor, plants, trees, and *all* living things need to drink water.

Just as our bodies need water to live on earth, we need *Jesus* in order to live with Him in His Heaven someday. Jesus said I have "Living Water" to give you. A, B

Water + soap make us and other things clean. Our hearts NEED a good cleaning every day too! C We clean our hearts by telling Jesus *every day* that we are sorry for our sins.

Treasure Talk: We need Jesus more than our bodies need water.

 DIG DEEPER

A John 7:37-38
B John 4:14
C Heb. 10:22

Take a drink of water right now. After you drink, say "Jesus, that water tastes so good. YOU taste even better! Please wash me clean from my sins."

Olive Tree

Not everyone likes those tiny, soft, egg-shaped green fruits with a red squishy thing in the middle. That's okay.

But, just so you know, olives are actually very healthy.

They are like vitamins that help our hearts, bones, and brains.

When Jesus was on earth, a long time before electricity was invented, people burned olive oil in lamps to get light.
David, a friend of God who wrote *many* Bible treasures, says, "I am like an olive tree."

A

Olive trees are very strong.

Olives mean *peace* and *life.* When Noah was on that HUGE boat, he sent out a dove,

and it came back with an *olive leaf* in its beak.   B The flood waters were at peace again.

> Even if you don't like olives, let's be like *that* kind of tree.
> And let our roots go deep in Jesus.

Treasure Talk: Ask God to help you be like a strong, peaceful olive tree.

A Psalm 52:8-9
B Gen 8:11

If there are olives in your refrigerator right now, take one out. You don't have to eat it, but pray: "Lord, please make me strong like an olive tree and help me to be like light so other people will know You!"

Wearing the Right Clothes?

Victor doesn't have to worry about what he wears. God gave him a hairy coat that never wears out.

But as *people* we must *take off* and *put on* clothes every day. Clothes cover us up, protect us, and keep us warm. If they get dirty, they get washed.

So many times in His Bible Jesus uses clothing treasure talk to tell us how to live! He explains what to get *rid of* in our lives—take off—and what to *add* to our lives—put on. These two actions will keep Jesus smiling and keeps us thinking about Him more than anything else!

Here are those actions:

#1 **Take off** lying, meanness, anger, swearing 🪏A, B

#2 **Take off** being jealous or saying unkind things about others 🪏C

#3 **Put on** a new self 🪏D

#4 **Put on** God's armor 🪏E

 #5 **Put on** Jesus 🪏F

Treasure Talk: Take off old habits; put on new ones.

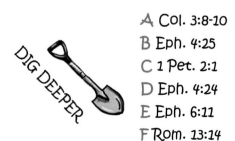

A Col. 3:8-10
B Eph. 4:25
C 1 Pet. 2:1
D Eph. 4:24
E Eph. 6:11
F Rom. 13:14

Next time you put on a shirt or pants or dress, ask yourself if you're "putting on" Jesus too! (The next page will talk about that "armor")

Protect Yourself

Armor protects! Soldiers and the police wear armor.

God gave some animals *armor* for protection: turtles have hard shells that shield them from danger; the armadillo has a name that means "little armored one" in Spanish.

The Creator God Who gave animals protection, uses this word to put a picture in our minds of how *we* can protect ourselves from our enemy--Satan!

As soldiers for Jesus we have to pray our armor on!

That may sound silly, but God tells us to do that.

These verses are written out in "Dig Deeper" in the back of this book, but this Treasure is also written here today:

"Wear the full armor of God. Wear God's armor so that you can fight against the devil's evil tricks. Our fight is not against people on earth...We are fighting against the spiritual powers of evil... That is why you need to get God's full armor. Then on the day of evil you will be able to stand strong. And when you have finished the whole fight, you will still be standing. So stand strong, with the belt of truth tied around your waist. And on your chest wear the protection of right living. And on your feet wear the Good News of peace to help you stand strong. And also use the shield of faith. With that you can stop all the burning arrows of the Evil One. Accept God's salvation to be your helmet. And take the sword of the Spirit—that sword is the teaching of God. Pray in the Spirit at all times. Pray with all kinds of prayers and ask for everything you need. To do this you must always be ready. Never give up. Always pray for all God's people." ⚒A

Treasure Talk: Live like a soldier with your God-armor on.

A Eph. 6:11-18

Ask an adult to find a large picture of an armored soldier. Write on each piece of armor the name that God gives it! For example, on the helmet write "salvation". If there are any words you do not understand, ask Mom, Dad, G'ma or G'pa. When you are done write "PRAY" in BIG black letters over top of the whole soldier!

March on, Soldier of Jesus!

Got Your Truth On?

One-by one we're going to discover the treasure of each piece of armor that protects us from Satan.

Paul is the Jesus-follower in the Bible who wrote about that armor we need to wear. Paul saw *real* soldiers every day who were walking around in that clanging metal suit.

He must have thought, "Hmm, that armor protects that man. It puts a picture in my mind of how I can protect myself against Satan's lies and tricks."

So Paul began with the soldier's **belt**. ⚒A
The belt was *wrapped around* the soldier's waist and held other pieces of armor tightly in place. That long, thin holder for the sword was also attached to the belt. A soldier could *not* go into battle without his sword!

Paul calls it the belt of *truth* because the Bible is God's truth to us. If we *know* God's true words and *wrap it around* our hearts and minds, it protects us and guards us

against Satan's lies. ⚒B

With heavy armor on, the soldier stood straight and could not be easily knocked over.

When the Bible says, "Stand strong," ⚒A that is treasure talk for "Don't let *anyone* fool you and tell you the Bible is not true!"

Treasure Talk: Let God's truth *wrap around* every thought or action.

A Eph. 6:14
B John 17:15-17

Talk this over with an adult you love: what are some of Satan's lies?

38

Making Right Choices

Paul said to wear on your chest the protection of right living. 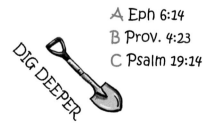A That means *make right choices.*

Every day you have the **choice** to listen to God's truth or to Satan's lies.

Every day you have the **choice** to do or say what is *right* or to do or say what is *wrong*.

A soldier (or the police) wears an extra heavy vest over the chest.

Inside the chest is the heart. The heart must be safe!

In treasure-talk, if you have a heart that mixes up recipes for doing what is right,

then you are making God smile! B, C

Treasure Talk: As a Christian soldier, guard your heart by making right choices that put a smile on God's face!

DIG DEEPER

A Eph 6:14
B Prov. 4:23
C Psalm 19:14

For one whole day make a list of the choices you make: food, clothes, toys, friends.
Now make a list of things you decided to DO or SAY that day?
Did your choices please Jesus?

Ready, Set, Go!

Have you ever heard this question: "Are you ready yet?" Have you ever answered by saying, "Almost. I just have to get my shoes on!"

It seems as though *shoes* make us *ready*. They protect our feet. They help us run faster or jump higher. They make us *look* ready for the day.

Football players, soccer players, or baseball players don't wear flip flops!

They wouldn't be *ready* for the game. They'd sit on the bench watching their teammates who *were* ready with proper shoes.

A very important piece of a soldier's armor was his shoes or boots. They had bumps on the bottom so they could run on rocky ground and not slip. They were *ready* for battle!

Our battle is against Satan. Paul, our Bible guide for Christian soldiers like us, says,

"Be **ready** to share why you love Jesus!" A It's another way to make Satan sad and God jumping-up-and-down–happy!

Treasure Talk: Are you ready—*really* ready—to talk about Jesus! B

A Eph. 6:15
B 1 Pet. 3:15

Practice telling Dad or Mom why you love Jesus. That will help to make you feel READY to tell other people!

You're Covered

God created a hard shell to cover and protect the soft bodies of turtles, armadillos, clams, crabs, and snails. Those hard shells are always with them—stuck to their bodies. They go wherever the animal goes. Those shells are like a shield from danger.

When it rains you may choose to carry an umbrella to protect you from getting sopping wet. You have to *decide* whether to carry it or not. An umbrella doesn't just pop out of your head!

In our armor treasure talk, Paul says to carry your "shield of faith". A

But it is a choice!

When you are sad or worried, do you still *know* that Jesus loves you and will keep all His promises? Do you pray about those things? *Then you have picked up the shield of faith!* You found the treasure that Satan, our enemy, was hoping you wouldn't find! You're covered! You're protected! You made a GOOD choice to believe!

Treasure Talk: Make the *choice* to carry the shield of your faith.

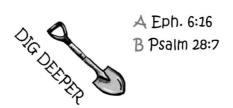

A Eph. 6:16
B Psalm 28:7

In Dig Deeper

Read Psalm 28:7. B
Now make up a song thanking God for always helping you. Sing it LOUD! Good job, Soldier!

41

What Are You Thinking?

You wear a helmet when you ride your bike in order to protect your head in case you fall. Football and hockey players wear helmets for the same reason.

As a Christian soldier we must wear a helmet to protect our *thoughts.* A
That may sound silly, but that is *exactly* what God wants us to do. It's an invisible helmet. This "invisible helmet" is a *thought* to protect our *thoughts!*
If a bad thought comes into your mind about other people, about doing something you know is wrong, or even about yourself, kick it out of your mind by saying, "NO! Jesus is what I want to think about! Jesus saved me from my sins! Jesus made me

and He's my Best Friend!" B
When we think <u>most</u> about Jesus and what He did for us by dying on a cross and rising again from the dead, well, that thought takes the place of ANY bad thought that

Satan tries to put in our heads! C

Treasure Talk: Thoughts about Jesus protect your mind like a helmet. You get to *choose* what you will think about.

A Eph. 6:17
B 1 Thess. 5:8
C Is. 12:2

With help and permission
Stick a piece of paper on your bike helmet that says:
"Jesus is my Helmet!"
Then you get to tell people what that means!

Stay Sharp

A dull knife does not carve a turkey well. A dull saw blade makes a mess out of a board Dad needs to cut. These things must be *sharp* in order to work well.

By now you know that we are in a fight against Satan who tries to get us to sin. A real soldier would NEVER go into battle without his sword.
As a *Christian* soldier, NEVER fight Satan without knowing God's words!

Your **sword** is God's W**ord**. God's Word is the Bible. ⚒A

> Since God's words are the last thing Satan wants to hear,
> it's the *first* thing we want to know and use!

So how "sharp" is *your* "sword"? That means: how well do you know God's words?

⚒B

Treasure Talk: Knowing verses from God's Word makes you a *sharp* Christian soldier.

A Eph. 6:17
B Heb. 4:12

These verses will get you started:
#1 "Trust in the Lord with all your heart."
    Proverbs 3:5
#2 "When I am afraid, I will trust in You."
    Psalm 56:3
#3_____

_____

_____

Pray It On

This is the eighth day of hearing about getting dressed in God's armor. By now you know that this armor is invisible, but it is THE MOST IMPORTANT six pieces of "clothing" you will *ever* "wear"! How do we wear something invisible?

We pray it on! We talk to God and ask Him to help us: 🪏 𝔸

Be truthful	*Make right choices*	*Talk about Jesus to others*
Cover ourselves with faith	*Choose good thoughts*	*Memorize Bible verses.*

When you were a baby you couldn't get dressed by yourself. Mom or Dad did it for you. You looked great! They didn't put your shoes on your ears. Your shirt went over your arms; your pants went over your legs and not the other way around.

As Christian soldiers, when we *pray* for God's help to get our armor on, He's going to help us in *just* the right way. That is a promise! Let's Dig Deeper right here on this page (AND in the back of the book). God's Word is SO POWERFUL! It's our weapon against Satan!

🪏𝔹 **2 Corinthians 10:3-5 (ICB)---"We do live in the world. But we do not fight in the same way that the world fights. We fight with weapons that are different from those the world uses. Our weapons have power from God. These weapons can destroy the enemy's strong places... And we destroy every proud thing that raises itself against the knowledge of God. We capture every thought and make it give up and obey Christ."**

Treasure Talk: Only God can help you wear your armor well. Ask Him!

𝔸 Eph. 6:18
𝔹 2 Cor. 10:3-5

Before your feet touch the floor in the morning, pray to God that He will help you put your armor on! Make this a habit.

It's a Race To The Finish

Victor can walk at about the same speed as you can. But when it comes to running, he is *much* faster.

Donkeys don't usually race, but they have carried heavy loads on very skinny roads. They do not stumble easily.

A treasure in the Bible says living on this earth is like running a *race*!

🔨A [Read this now!]

Here is what we know about running a good race:	Here is the treasure talk when the *Bible* says to run a "race":
#1 Wear good shoes so you don't slip>>	>>remember HOW God wants you to act and live.
#2 Don't wear heavy clothes>>>>>>>	>>ask God to take away your sins.
#3 Stay on the path>>>>>>>>>>>>	>>Satan doesn't want you on Jesus' path. Tell him to get lost!
#4 If outside, watch out for bumps>>>	>>there WILL be troubles in life...but God will help you get around them or through them.
#5 Look forward to the finish>>>>>>>	>>keep thinking *only* about Jesus B
#6 People on the sides cheer you on>>>	>>people who know and love Jesus are *always* your "cheerleaders" to help you in this race. Let them!

Treasure Talk: God is beside us, behind us and ahead of us in this life.

A Heb. 12:1
B Heb. 12:2

Think of ways *you* can cheer people on to run the best race for Jesus!
What is our "finish line?

H _ _ _ _ N

Now read this: "I have finished the race. I have kept the faith." (2 Tim. 4:7)

[spelling hint: HEAVEN]

We're On A Trip

Has Dad or Mom ever said, "We're going on a trip! Get your bags packed!
It will be an adventure!"?

That is exactly what the Bible calls our life when we love Jesus. It's like **He** is the
"Driver" or the "Trip Planner" or the "Adventure Guide."

On a road trip with Dad or Mom we may have a rain storm or a flat tire along the way.
That slows things up, but then we move on.

As we live for Jesus, there are often those yucky times that we could call "storms" or
"flat tires." But by praying about them, God will help us get through them or around
them.

Then the adventure with Him continues. 🪧A, B

On this life trip, Jesus is with us all the way. He will *never* leave us. 🪧C **NEVER!**

When Dad or Mom are driving, you feel safe enough to fall asleep. You are *trusting*
them.

Are you trusting God every day? 🪧D

If we worry too much about that yucky stuff, then we are not trusting enough.

Treasure Talk: In this adventure called life, trust God.

A 1 Cor.1:9
B Phil. 1:6
C Deut. 31:6
D Prov. 3:5-6

Things you need
to pack for a
trip:
Toothbrush
Rain Gear
Ice
Pajamas

Things to remember
in this cool trip called
life:
Trust God
Read about Him
Invite Jesus along
Pray

Solid as a Rock

What do you think of when you hear that word, "rock"?

You can't squish it in your hands like a soft rubber ball.
If it's too big, it's hard to pick up or move.

Now think HUGE--imagine a rock as big as your house.

THAT can't be moved! THAT can't be held!

THAT rock is going nowhere. THAT is like our Great Big God! A, C

He's staying with you. He will *never* move away. B

Now THAT puts a picture in our minds. God ALWAYS loves you. God is ALWAYS there for you when you need Him. You can ALWAYS trust Him.

Treasure Talk: God is *always* with us.

A Deut. 32:4
B Deut. 31:6
C 1 Sam. 2:2

Find a small rock with a flat top.
Stand on it. Did you ruin it?
Now stand on a pile of sand or dirt.
What happened?
Say out loud: "Thank you, God, for being my very own Solid Rock!"

A Prayer To Choose God Forever!

Dear God, I want You to live in my heart forever! I am very sorry for all that I do wrong. You call it sin, Lord, and I am sorry for those sins. I believe that You sent Jesus to die on a cross in order to pay for all my sins. I believe He is making a place for me in heaven. Thank you for loving me and for knocking at the door of my heart. Today I invite You in to stay forever!

Help me, please, to wear Your armor every day.

In Jesus Name, Amen.

Bible verses are from one of these versions:
The Message (MSG)
The International Children's Bible (ICB)
The New International Version (NIV)
The New Living Translation (NLT)
New King James Version (NKJV)
Amplified Bible (AMP)
Common English Bible (CEB)
Contemporary English Version (CEV)

Page 3, Victor the Donkey

Luke 19:28-40 (MSG) Jesus headed straight up to Jerusalem. When he got near Bethphage and Bethany at the mountain called Olives, he sent off two of the disciples with instructions: "Go to the village across from you. As soon as you enter, you'll find a colt tethered, one that has never been ridden. Untie it and bring it. If anyone says anything, asks, 'What are you doing?' say, 'His Master needs him.'"
The two left and found it just as he said. As they were untying the colt, its owners said, "What are you doing untying the colt?"
They said, "His Master needs him."
They brought the colt to Jesus. Then, throwing their coats on its back, they helped Jesus get on. As he rode, the people gave him a grand welcome, throwing their coats on the street.
Right at the crest, where Mount Olives begins its descent, the whole crowd of disciples burst into enthusiastic praise over all the mighty works they had witnessed:
Blessed is he who comes, the king in God's name!
All's well in heaven! Glory in the high places!
Some Pharisees from the crowd told him, "Teacher, get your disciples under control!"
But he said, "If they kept quiet, the stones would do it for them, shouting praise."

Page 4, You Are God's Treasure!

Psalm 139:1-6 (ICB) "Lord, you have examined me. You know all about me.
You know when I sit down and when I get up. You know my thoughts before I think them. You know where I go and where I lie down. You know well everything I do. Lord, even before I say a word, you already know what I am going to say. You are all around me—in front and in back. You have put your hand on me. Your knowledge is amazing to me.
It is more than I can understand."

Page 5, Is God Your Treasure?

A Matthew 6:19-21 (MSG) "Don't hoard treasure down here where it gets eaten by moths and corroded by rust or—worse!—stolen by burglars. Stockpile treasure in heaven, where it's safe from moth and rust and burglars. It's obvious, isn't it? The place where your treasure is, is the place you will most want to be, and end up being."
B Matthew 13:44-46 (ICB) "The kingdom of heaven is like a treasure hidden in a field. One day a man found the treasure, and then he hid it in the field again. The man was very happy to find the treasure. He went and sold everything that he owned to buy that field.

Also, the kingdom of heaven is like a man looking for fine pearls. One day he found a very valuable pearl. The man went and sold everything he had to buy that pearl."

Page 6, Shoulders Are For Resting

A Deuteronomy 33:12 (NIV) "... the one the LORD loves rests between his shoulders."

B Psalm 55:22 (MSG) "Pile your troubles on GOD's shoulders—He'll carry your load, He'll help you out."

C Matthew 11:28 (CEB) "Come to me, all you who are struggling hard and carrying heavy loads, and I will give you rest."

Page 7, Shoulders (again)

A Job 12:7-9 (ICB) "But ask the animals, and they will teach you, or the birds in the sky, and they will tell you; or speak to the earth, and it will teach you, or let the fish in the sea inform you. Which of all these does not know that the hand of the Lord has done this?"

B Revelation 22:16 (ICB) "I, Jesus, have sent my angel to tell you...I am the bright morning star."

C Philippians 2:8-11 (ICB) "And when he [Jesus] was living as a man, he humbled himself and was fully obedient to God. He obeyed even when that caused his death—death on a cross. So, God raised Christ to the highest place. God made the name of Christ greater than every other name. God wants every knee to bow to Jesus—everyone in heaven, on earth, and under the earth. Everyone will say, 'Jesus Christ is Lord' and bring glory to God the Father."

Page 8, Obey Road Signs

A Numbers 22:21-35 (ICB) "Balaam got up the next morning. He put a saddle on his donkey.... But God became angry because Balaam went. So the angel of the Lord stood in the road to stop Balaam. Balaam was riding his donkey... The donkey saw the angel of the Lord standing in the road...So the donkey left the road and went into the field. Balaam hit the donkey to force her back on the road.
Later, the angel of the Lord stood on a narrow path between two vineyards. There were walls on both sides. Again the donkey saw the angel of the Lord. So the donkey walked close to one wall. This crushed Balaam's foot against the wall. So he hit her again.
The angel of the Lord went ahead again. The angel stood at a narrow place. It was too narrow to turn left or right. The donkey saw the angel of the Lord. So she lay down under Balaam. Balaam was very angry and hit her with his stick. Then the Lord made the donkey talk. She said to Balaam, "What have I done to make you hit me three times?"
Balaam answered the donkey, "You have made me look foolish...!"
But the donkey said to Balaam, "I am your very own donkey. You have ridden me for years. Have I ever done this to you before?"
"No," Balaam said.
Then the Lord let Balaam see the angel...Then Balaam bowed face down on the ground.
The angel of the Lord asked Balaam, "Why have you hit your donkey three times? I have stood here to stop you. What you are doing is wrong. The donkey saw me...
Then Balaam said to the angel of the Lord, "I have sinned. I did not know you were standing in the road to stop me. If I am wrong, I will go back."
The angel of the Lord said to Balaam, "Go with these men. But say only what I tell you." So Balaam went..."

B Psalm 19:11 (MSG) "...God's Word warns us of danger and directs us to hidden treasure."

Page 9, We Are Clay Pots

A Jeremiah 18:3-4 (ICB) "So I went down to the potter's house. I saw him working at the potter's wheel. He was making a pot from clay. But something went wrong with it. So the potter used that clay to make another pot. He used his hands to shape the pot the way that he wanted it to be."

B Psalm 139:13-16 (ICB) "You made my whole being. You formed me in my mother's body. I praise you because you made me in an amazing and wonderful way.
What you have done is wonderful. I know this very well.
You saw my bones being formed as I took shape in my mother's body.
When I was put together there, you saw my body as it was formed.
All the days planned for me were written in your book before I was one day old."

Page 10, We Are Cracked Clay Pots

1 John 1:9 (CEV) "But if we confess our sins to God, he can always be trusted to forgive us and take our sins away."

Page 11, I Am His Sheep

A Psalm 100:3 (ICB) "Know that the Lord is God. He made us, and we belong to him.
We are his people, the sheep he tends.

B John 10:11 (ICB) "I am the good shepherd. The good shepherd gives his life for the sheep."

C Job 34:21 (ICB) "God watches where people go. He sees every step they take."

Page 12, Sheep Habits

A Psalm 23:1 (ICB) "The Lord is my Shepherd. I have everything I need."

B Hebrews 13:5,6 (MSG) "God assured us, "I'll never let you down, never walk off and leave you, we can boldly quote, God is there, ready to help..."

C John 10:27 (ICB) "My sheep listen to my voice. I know them, and they follow me."

D John 10:3 (ICB) "And the sheep listen to the voice of the shepherd. He calls his own sheep, using their names, and he leads them out."

E Jeremiah 15:16 (NIV) "When your words came, I ate them; they were my joy and my heart's delight, for I bear your name, LORD God Almighty."

F Luke 15:3-7 (ICB) "Then Jesus told them this story: "Suppose one of you has 100 sheep, but he loses 1 of them. Then he will leave the other 99 sheep alone and go out and look for the lost sheep. The man will keep on searching for the lost sheep until he finds it. And when he finds it, the man is very happy. He puts it on his shoulders and goes home. He calls to his friends and neighbors and says, 'Be happy with me because I found my lost sheep!' In the same way, I tell you there is much joy in heaven when 1 sinner changes his heart. There is more joy for that 1 sinner than there is for 99 good people who don't need to change."

Page 13, Tricky Wolf

A John 8:44 (ICB) "...the devil...there is no truth in him. He is a liar, and he is like the lies he tells. He is the father of lies."

B John 14:6 (MSG) "Jesus said, "I am the Road, also the Truth, also the Life."

Page 14, The Trusty Gate

A Psalm 100:3 (ICB) "...we are his people, the sheep he tends."

B Luke 12:32 (ICB) "Don't fear, little flock. Your Father wants to give you the kingdom."
C John 10:9, 10 (MSG) "I am the Gate for the sheep. All those others are up to no good—sheep stealers, every one of them. But the sheep didn't listen to them. I am the Gate. Anyone who goes through me will be cared for—will freely go in and out, and find pasture. A thief is only there to steal and kill and destroy. I came so they can have real and eternal life, more and better life than they ever dreamed of."

Page 15, A Work of Art

A Ephesians 2:10 (NLT) "For we are God's masterpiece."
B Psalm 139:14-16 (ICB) "I praise you because you made me in an amazing and wonderful way. What you have done is wonderful. I know this very well.
You saw my bones being formed as I took shape in my mother's body.
When I was put together there, you saw my body as it was formed.
All the days planned for me were written in your book before I was one day old."

Page 16, Look At The Birds

A Matthew 6:26 (ICB) "Look at the birds in the air. They don't plant or harvest or store food in barns. But your heavenly Father feeds the birds. And you know that you are worth much more than the birds."
B Matthew 10:29-30 (NLT) "But not a single sparrow can fall to the ground without your Father knowing it. And the very hairs on your head are all numbered."

Page 17, A Loud Cluck and Strong Wings

Matthew 23:37 (NLT) "How often I have wanted to gather your children together as a hen protects her chicks beneath her wings..."

Page 18, Your Safe Place!

A Psalm 94:22 (MSG) "...God became my hideout; God was my high mountain retreat.."
B Psalm 91:4,9 (MSG) "His huge outstretched arms protect you— under them you're perfectly safe; his arms fend off all harm. Fear nothing...Yes, because GOD's your refuge,
the High God your very own home."
C Hebrews 13:5,6 (MSG) "'I'll never let you down, never walk off and leave you,'...God is there, ready to help; I'm fearless no matter what. Who or what can get to me?"

Page 19, Dwelling Place

A, C Ephesians 2:22 (NIV) "And in him you too are being built together to become a dwelling in which God lives by his Spirit."
B John 14:2-3 (AMP) "In My Father's house are many dwelling places. If it were not so, I would have told you, because I am going there to prepare a place for you. And if I go and prepare a place for you, I will come back again and I will take you to Myself, so that where I am you may be also."

Page 20, Just Like Tents

A 2 Corinthians 5:1 (CEV) "Our bodies are like tents that we live in here on earth. But when these tents are destroyed, we know that God will give each of us a place to live. These homes will not be buildings that someone has made, but they are in heaven and will last forever."

B John 14:2 (AMP) "In My Father's house are many dwelling places. If it were not so, I would have told you, because I am going there to prepare a place for you."

Page 21, Vines and Branches

John 15:5-8 (CEV) "I am the vine, and you are the branches. If you stay joined to me, and I stay joined to you, then you will produce lots of fruit. But you cannot do anything without me. If you don't stay joined to me, you will be thrown away. You will be like dry branches that are gathered up and burned in a fire. Stay joined to me and let my teachings become part of you. Then you can pray for whatever you want, and your prayer will be answered. When you become fruitful disciples of mine, my Father will be honored."

Page 22, Tree Talk

A Psalm 1:2-3 (MSG) "...you thrill to GOD's Word, you chew on Scripture day and night. You're a tree...bearing fresh fruit every month, never dropping a leaf, always in blossom."
B Colossians 2:6-7 (ICB) "As you received Christ Jesus the Lord, so continue to live in him. Keep your roots deep in him and have your lives built on him. Be strong in the faith, just as you were taught. And always be thankful."

Page 23, Be Fruity

A Proverbs 20:11 (CEV) "The good or bad that children do shows what they are like."
B Galatians 5:22 (NIV) "But the fruit of the Spirit is love, joy, peace, patience, kindness, goodness, faithfulness, gentleness and self-control. Against such things there is no law."
C Matthew 7:16 (NKJV) "You will know them by their fruits."

Page 24, Strong, Deep Roots

Jeremiah 17:7,8 (ICB) "But the person who trusts in the Lord will be blessed.
The Lord will show him that he can be trusted. He will be strong, like a tree planted near water. That tree has large roots that find the water. It is not afraid when the days are hot. Its leaves are always green. It does not worry in a year when no rain comes.
That tree always produces fruit."

Page 25, Your Heart Has Eyes and Ears

A Matthew 13:16 (CEV) "But God has blessed you, because your eyes can see and your ears can hear!"
B Luke 6:45 (ICB) "A good person has good things saved up in his heart. And so he brings good things out of his heart... A person speaks the things that are in his heart."

Page26, Honey

Proverbs 16:24 (CEV) "Kind words are like honey—they cheer you up and make you feel strong."

Page 27, Bright With Light

A John 8:12 (NIV) "I am the light of the world. Whoever follows me will never walk in darkness but will have the light of life."
B John 1:5 (CEV) "The light keeps shining in the dark, and darkness has never put it out."

Page 28, What Path Are You On?

A Psalm 119:105 (CEV) "Your word is a lamp that gives light wherever I walk."
B Hebrews 12:2 (CEV) "We must keep our eyes on Jesus, who leads us and makes our faith complete."
C Luke 1:79 (MSG) "[God] then showing us the way, one foot at a time, down the path of peace."
D Psalm 23:3 (CEV) "...you lead me along the right paths."

Page 29, Hide It!

A Psalm 119:11 (NIV) "I have hidden your word in my heart that I might not sin against you."
B Proverbs 2:1-5 (CEV) "My child, you must follow and treasure my teachings and my instructions... Search for wisdom as you would search for silver or hidden treasure. Then you will understand what it means to respect and to know the LORD God."

Page 30, Jesus Is Your Ladder

A John 14:6 (CEV) "I am the way, the truth, and the life!" Jesus answered. "Without me, no one can go to the Father."
B John 1:51 (ICB) "And Jesus said to them, "I tell you the truth. You will all see heaven open. You will see angels of God going up and coming down on the Son of Man."
C Genesis 28:12 (ICB) "Jacob dreamed that there was a ladder resting on the earth and reaching up into heaven. And he saw angels of God going up and coming down the ladder."

Page 31, God and Gold

A 1 Peter 1:7 (NIV) "...your faith—of greater worth than gold..."
B Psalm 19:9,10 (CEV) "...All of his decisions are correct and fair. They are worth more than the finest gold..."
C Proverbs 16:16 (ICB) "It is better to get wisdom than gold."
D Revelation 21:21(ICB) "The street of the city was made of pure gold. The gold was clear as glass."
E Job 22:25 (MSG) "God Almighty will be your treasure..."

Page 32, Rope and Anchor

A Hebrews 6:18-19 (CEV) "We have run to God for safety. Now his promises should greatly encourage us to take hold of the hope that is right in front of us. This hope is like a firm and steady anchor for our souls."

Page 33, Don't Forget The Soap

A Genesis 43:24 (ICB) "The servant...gave them water, and they washed their feet. Then he gave their donkeys food to eat."
B Psalm 51:7 (MSG) "Soak me in your laundry and I'll come out clean, scrub me and I'll have a snow-white life."
C Leviticus 17:11 (ICB) "It is the blood that removes the sins from your life so you will belong to the Lord."
D Malachi 3:2,3 (CEV) "On the day the Lord comes, he will be like...strong soap in a washbasin. No one will be able to stand up to him. The LORD will purify..."

E Matthew 25:21 (ICB) "The master answered, 'You did well. You are a good servant... Come and share my happiness with me.'"

Page 34, Living Water

A John 7:37-38 (ICB) "Jesus stood up and said in a loud voice, 'If anyone is thirsty, let him come to me and drink. If a person believes in me, rivers of living water will flow out from his heart.'"

B John 4:14 (ICB) "But whoever drinks the water I give will never be thirsty again. The water I give will become a spring of water flowing inside him. It will give him eternal life."

C Hebrews 10:12 (ICB) "So let us come near to God with a sincere heart and a sure faith. We have been cleansed and made free from feelings of guilt."

Page 35, Olive Tree

A Psalm 52:8-9 (CEV) "But I am like an olive tree growing in God's house, and I can count on his love forever and ever. I will always thank God for what he has done; I will praise his good name..."

B Genesis 8:11 (CEV) "It [the dove] returned in the evening, holding in its beak a green leaf from an olive tree. Noah knew that the water was finally going down." (emphasis mine)

Page 36, Wearing The Right Clothes?

A Colossians 3:8-10 (MSG) "But you know better now, so make sure it's all gone for good: bad temper, irritability, meanness, profanity, dirty talk. Don't lie to one another. You're done with that old life. It's like a filthy set of ill-fitting clothes you've stripped off and put in the fire. Now you're dressed in a new wardrobe. Every item of your new way of life is custom-made by the Creator, with his label on it."

B Ephesians 4:25 (ICB) "So you must stop telling lies. Tell each other the truth..."

C 1 Peter 2:1 (CEV) "Don't be jealous or say cruel things about others."

D Ephesians 4:24 (NIV) "...put on the new self, created to be like God in true righteousness [right living] and holiness." (emphasis mine)

E Ephesians 6:11 (ICB) "Wear the full armor of God. Wear God's armor so that you can fight against the devil's evil tricks."

F Romans 13:14 (CEV) "Let the Lord Jesus Christ be as near to you as the clothes you wear. Then you won't try to satisfy your selfish desires."

Page 37, Protect Yourself

A Ephesians 6:11-18 (ICB) "Wear the full armor of God. Wear God's armor so that you can fight against the devil's evil tricks. Our fight is not against people on earth...We are fighting against the spiritual powers of evil...That is why you need to get God's full armor. Then on the day of evil you will be able to stand strong. And when you have finished the whole fight, you will still be standing. So stand strong, with the belt of truth tied around your waist. And on your chest wear the protection of right living. And on your feet wear the Good News of peace to help you stand strong. And also use the shield of faith. With that you can stop all the burning arrows of the Evil One. Accept God's salvation to be your helmet. And take the sword of the Spirit—that sword is the teaching of God. Pray in the Spirit at all times. Pray with all kinds of prayers, and ask for everything you need. To do this you must always be ready. Never give up. Always pray for all God's people."

Page 38, Got Your Truth On?

A Ephesians 6:14 (ICB) "So stand strong, with the belt of truth tied around your waist."
B John 17:15-17 (CEV) "Father...keep them safe from the evil one. They don't belong to this world, and neither do I. Your word is the truth. So let this truth make them completely yours."

Page 39, Making Right Choices

A Ephesians 6:14 (ICB) "So stand strong, with the belt of truth tied around your waist. And on your chest wear the protection of right living."
B Proverbs 4:23 (NIV) "Above all else, guard your heart, for everything you do flows from it."
C Psalm 19:14 (CEV) "Let my words and my thoughts be pleasing to you, LORD, because you are my mighty rock and my protector."

Page 40, Ready, Set, Go!

A Ephesians 6:15 (CEB) "...put shoes on your feet so that you are ready to spread the good news of peace."
B 1 Peter 3:15 (CEV) "Honor Christ and let him be the Lord of your life. Always be ready to give an answer when someone asks you about your hope."

Page 41, You're Covered

A Ephesians 6:16 (CEB) "Above all, carry the shield of faith..."
B Psalm 28:7 (CEV) "You are my strong shield, and I trust you completely. You have helped me, and I will celebrate and thank you in song."

Page 42, What Are You Thinking?

A Ephesians 6:17 (ICB) "Accept God's salvation to be your helmet."
B 1 Thessalonians 5:8 (CEV) "Our firm hope that we will be saved is our helmet."
C Isaiah 12:2 (CEV) "I trust you to save me, LORD God, and I won't be afraid. My power and my strength come from you, and you have saved me."

Page 43, Stay Sharp

A Ephesians 6:17 (CEB) "Take... the sword of the Spirit, which is God's word."
B Hebrews 4:12 (CEV) "What God has said isn't only alive and active! It is sharper than any double-edged sword."

Page 44, Pray It On

A Ephesians 6:18 (MSG) "...prayer is essential in this ongoing warfare. Pray hard and long."
B 2 Corinthians 10:3-5 (ICB) "We do live in the world. But we do not fight in the same way that the world fights. We fight with weapons that are different from those the world uses. Our weapons have power from God. These weapons can destroy the enemy's strong places. We destroy men's arguments. And we destroy every proud thing that raises itself against the knowledge of God. We capture every thought and make it give up and obey Christ."

Page 45, It's A Race To The Finish

A Hebrews 12:1 (ICB) "So we have many people of faith around us. Their lives tell us what faith means. So let us run the race that is before us and never give up. We should remove from our lives anything that would get in the way. And we should remove the sin that so easily catches us."

B Hebrews 12:2 (ICB) "Let us look only to Jesus. He is the one who began our faith, and he makes our faith perfect."

Page 46, We're On A Trip

A 1 Corinthians 1:9 (MSG) "God himself is right alongside to keep you steady and on track until things are all wrapped up by Jesus. God, who got you started in this spiritual adventure, shares with us the life of his Son and our Master Jesus. He will never give up on you. Never forget that."

B Philippians1:6 (ICB) "God began doing a good work in you. And he will continue it until it is finished when Jesus Christ comes again. I am sure of that."

C Deuteronomy 31:6 (ICB) "Be strong and brave. Don't be afraid... Don't be frightened. The Lord your God will go with you. He will not leave you or forget you."

D Proverbs 3:5-6 (MSG) "Trust GOD from the bottom of your heart; don't try to figure out everything on your own. Listen for GOD's voice in everything you do, everywhere you go; he's the one who will keep you on track."

Page 47, Solid As A Rock

A Deuteronomy 32:4 (ICB) "He is like a rock. What he does is perfect. He is always fair. He is a faithful God who does no wrong. He is right and fair."

B Deuteronomy 31:6 (ICB) "...He will not leave you or forget you."

C 1 Samuel 2:2 (ICB) "There is no one holy like the Lord. There is no God but you. There is no Rock like our God."

 Like Victor's Facebook page @victorthedonkey

57

About The Author

Sharon Deur is a daughter of the King of kings and loves helping children know they are royalty too. She graduated from Calvin University with a degree in elementary education. She taught preschool, kindergarten, second and fourth grades. She has led Bible Studies and Mom to Mom groups. She is a mentor for MOPS (Mothers of Preschoolers) and a trainer of Love and Logic® Curricula. Pilgrim's Progress, which Sharon read as a young teen, gave her a profound appreciation for Biblical imagery. She and her husband live in Michigan.

Sharon also wants you to know that you can Follow *Victor The Donkey* on Facebook at https://www.facebook.com/VictortheDonkey/ .

Victor Discovers Treasure 2 is coming soon!

Made in the USA
Columbia, SC
04 September 2021

44664466R00038